Philippians Inductive Bible Study

"Overflowing Joy"

"Rejoice in the Lord always. Again I will say, rejoice!"

Philippians 4:4

Published By
Morningstar Christian Chapel
Whittier, California 90603

Philippians Inductive Bible Study
"Overflowing Joy"
Copyright © 2001
ISBN: 978-1-7224825-3-4
All rights reserved. No part of this book can be reproduced
in any form without written permission from the publisher.

Additional copies of this book are available by contacting:

Morningstar Christian Chapel
Whittier, California 90603
562.943.0297

Printed in the United States

Unless otherwise noted all Scripture quotations
are taken from the New King James Version,
Copyright © 1982 by Thomas Nelson, Inc.

Introduction

Philippians is a joyful letter, the happiest letter the Apostle Paul ever penned. It was written in 60-62 AD as a letter of thanks, a letter of encouragement and a reminder to the church at Philippi of the joy and rejoicing found in the Lord Jesus Christ.

Philippi was the first city on the continent of Europe in which the gospel of Jesus Christ was ever preached (Acts 16). The Lord used a night vision to reveal to Paul that he should go to Macedonia. The church began with the conversion of Lydia, a demon-possessed girl, and a jailer and his family.

It is easy to forget, when reading this letter, that Paul was in Rome under house arrest while he was writing, yet we hear no complaining, no bitterness, and no resentment — just rejoicing!

We might summarize the letter using one verse from each chapter:

> *What then? Notwithstanding, every way, whether in pretense, or in truth, Christ is preached; and I therein do* **rejoice***, yea, and will* **rejoice***. Philippians 1:18*
>
> *Yea, and if I be offered upon the sacrifice and service of your faith, I joy, and* **rejoice** *with you all. Philippians 2:17*
>
> *For we are the circumcision, which worship God in the spirit, and* **rejoice** *in Christ Jesus, and have no confidence in the flesh. Philippians 3:3*
>
> **Rejoice** *in the Lord always: and again I say,* **Rejoice***. Philippians 4:4*

Jesus was *"a Man of sorrows and acquainted with grief,"* yet He possessed a deep joy that was beyond anything the world could offer. He faced a certain, cruel death at Calvary, but said to His disciples, *"These things have I spoken unto you, that my joy might remain in you, and that* **your joy might be full***." John 15:11*

As a child of God, one whose life has been redeemed from sin

INTRODUCTION CONTINUED...

and death, the Christian is able to experience *"fullness of joy."* (Psalm 16:11)

Yet, the believer is sometimes robbed of this joy by circumstances, people, things or worry. There are a couple of other frequently repeated words in Paul's letter, they are: mind, think and remember. We will not experience the joy that is ours in the Lord Jesus Christ when we fail in our thoughts, attitudes and reactions.

According to the Apostle Paul the secret of true joy is found in the way a believer thinks:
"For as he thinks in his heart, so is he..." Proverbs 23:7

Let's turn the focus of our hearts and minds from the things of the world to those things which are eternal and we will experience joy unspeakable. (1 Peter 1:8)

May our Lord Jesus Christ richly bless you and fill you with joy as you study this little letter filled with a powerful message of the joy and rejoicing that is ours as children of God.

Study Outline

CHAPTER 1

Paul's counsel from close to the heart
His profound joy in prayer
   over their diligence in faith . . . . vs 1–11
His determination to preach Christ
   no matter the cost . . . . vs 12–18
His dilemma between being here and going there . . . vs 19–26

CHAPTER 2

Having the mind of Christ
Sharing with one another
   what you have received from Jesus . . . . vs 1–4
Following His example, His heart, His love . . . . vs 5–11
Lighting the path with the testimony of your life . . . vs 12–18
Words of commendations for
   Timothy and Epaphroditus . . . . vs 19–30

CHAPTER 3

Warnings about legalism and carnality
The lure of the law and the liberty of grace . . . . vs 1–11
Right on target . . . . vs 12–16
A citizen of heaven here on a visa . . . . vs 17–21

CHAPTER 4

I got that joy, joy, joy, joy...
The joy of having His peace . . . . vs 1–7
The joy of thinking on His word . . . . vs 8–9
The joy of faithful brethren . . . . vs 10–20
The joy of knowing Him . . . . vs 21–23

©2001—MORNINGSTAR CHRISTIAN CHAPEL, WHITTIER, CA

Lesson Index

LESSON	TEXT	PAGE
1	Philippians Overview	1
2	Philippians 1:1–11	5
3	Philippians 1:12–20	13
4	Philippians 1:21–30	23
5	Philippians 2:1–11	33
6	Philippians 2:12–18	43
7	Philippians 2:19–30	53
8	Philippians 3:1–11	63
9	Philippians 3:12–21	73
10	Philippians 4:1–9	83
11	Philippians 4:10–23	93

| PHILIPPIANS OVERVIEW | 1 | LESSON #1 |

Always begin every Bible Study in Prayer. It is the Holy Spirit Who teaches us and without Him we are only doing a memory exercise with no spiritual results!

DAY 1—BEGIN IN PRAYER

1. Read the complete Philippian letter and Acts 16:6–40.

2. **Who** are the writers? **Where** are they?

3. To **whom** are they writing?

4. **Where** is the city to which the letter is sent? (Find it on a Bible map, if possible).

5. **Why** do you think they are writing?

DAY 2—BEGIN IN PRAYER

1. Read the complete Philippian letter.

2. **What** are a few truths that were of great encouragement to you?

3. **What** were some of the warnings that are to be heeded?

overFLOWING joy

©2001—Morningstar Christian Chapel, Whittier, CA

PHILIPPIANS OVERVIEW

DAY 3—BEGIN IN PRAYER

1. Read Philippians 1.

2. What are the main subjects?

3. What are the key words? (Words used frequently and those that give us the main focus of the chapter.)

4. Can you choose a key verse for this chapter? (A verse that summarizes the chapter.)

5. What is the Lord teaching you today?

DAY 4—BEGIN IN PRAYER

1. Read Philippians 2.

2. What are the main subjects?

3. What are the key words?

4. Can you choose a key verse for this chapter?

5. What instruction is given that we should apply to our lives today?

DAY 5—BEGIN IN PRAYER

1. Read Philippians 3.

2. What are the main subjects?

3. What are the key words?

4. Can you choose a key verse for this chapter?

5. What is the lesson to be learned?

DAY 6—BEGIN IN PRAYER

1. Read Philippians 4.

2. What are the main subjects?

3. What are the key words?

| PHILIPPIANS OVERVIEW | 4 | LESSON #1 |

4. Can you choose a key verse for this chapter?

5. What is the lesson to be learned?

6. How has the Lord changed your heart through the study of Philippians this week?

For the Word of God is quick, and powerful, and sharper than any two-edged sword, piercing even to the dividing asunder of soul and spirit, and of the joints and marrow, and is a discerner of the thoughts and intents of the heart. Hebrews 4:12

PHILIPPIANS 1:1–11 — LESSON #2

DAY 1—BEGIN IN PRAYER

1. Read Philippians chapter 1.

2. Re-read Philippians 1:1–11.

3. What are the main topics in verses 1–11?

4. Choose a verse to memorize this week. Begin working on it now.

DAY 2—BEGIN IN PRAYER

1. Read Philippians 1:1–2.

2. As was customary in those days, Paul begins this short letter with his signature. He is writing to the saints (believers) at Philippi. How does he describe himself and Timothy?

   What vital words of blessing did he send to the Body of Christ in Philippi?

3. Look up the definitions of the following words. *(Use a Bible dictionary, Vines, Strong's Concordance or a regular English language dictionary.)*

    a. Servants (v. 1)

    b. Saints (v. 1)

overFLOWING joy

PHILIPPIANS 1:1–11 — LESSON #2

c. Grace (v. 2)

d. Peace (v. 2)

4. What more do we learn about grace and peace from the following Scriptures?

   a. 2Corinthians 9:8

   b. 2Corinthians 12:9

   c. Ephesians 2:8–9

   d. Ephesians 2:14–18

5. In today's lesson, what *instructions* do we need to follow? What *warnings* must we heed? Are there any *promises* we can rest our faith upon?

6. Close your study time in prayer asking the Lord Jesus to make any necessary changes in your heart, mind and attitude this week!

PHILIPPIANS 1:1-11 — LESSON #2

DAY 3—BEGIN IN PRAYER

1. Read Philippians 1:3-6.

2. Paul begins this letter by expressing his thanksgiving for the church at Philippi and declaring that he *"Always in every prayer made petition for them with joy."* Who are the people in your life for whom you are thankful? Does that thanksgiving cause you to joyfully pray for them often?

3. What do the following Scriptures teach us about prayer, the power of prayer and the value of being a faithful prayer warrior?

    a. Psalm 145:18, 19

    b. 1 Thessalonians 5:17

    c. 1 Timothy 2:1-3

    d. Ephesians 6:18, 19

    e. Philippians 4:6, 7

    f. James 5:16

PHILIPPIANS 1:1–11 — LESSON #2

4. The Philippians had stood by Paul, supported him, and followed him with their prayers. They had become partners in the Gospel. He greatly appreciated their fellowship and was certain that the work, which the Lord had begun in them, would be continued until His return. What do the following verses teach us about this same work of God's in the life of the Christian?

   a. 1 Peter 5:10

   b. Hebrews 12:1, 2

   c. Hebrews 13:20, 21

5. In today's lesson, what *instructions* do we need to follow? What *warnings* must we heed? Are there any *promises* we can rest our faith upon?

6. Close your study time in prayer asking the Lord Jesus to make any necessary changes in your heart, mind and attitude this week!

DAY 4—BEGIN IN PRAYER

1. Read Philippians 1:7–8.

2. Paul loved this church and was deeply concerned for its welfare. What phrases support this truth?

   a. (v. 7)

PHILIPPIANS 1:1–11 — LESSON #2

b. (v. 8)

3. Paul's confidence in the Philippian believers was based on solid evidence. They willingly supported him, not being afraid of the charge against him or the bondage of his imprisonment. The charge Paul faced because of his faithfulness to preach the Gospel was very serious, and to support a person accused of such crimes could easily bring about similar punishment. The following Scriptures would have been a source of encouragement to these early believers. How do they help you to boldly stand and proclaim the truth of the Gospel?

   a. Psalm 56:4

   b. Proverbs 29:25, 26

   c. Isaiah 51:7, 8

   d. Hebrews 13:5, 6

4. What do we learn from the following verses about the Christian love that was so evident in Paul's life?

   a. John 13:34, 35

   b. 1 John 3:14

c. 1 John 4:7

d. 1 Peter 3:8, 9

5. In today's lesson, what *instructions* do we need to follow? What *warnings* must we heed? Are there any *promises* we can rest our faith upon?

6. Close your study time in prayer asking the Lord Jesus to make any necessary changes in your heart, mind and attitude this week!

DAY 5—BEGIN IN PRAYER

1. Read Philippians 1:9-11.

2. What four things does Paul pray for the church?

   a.

   b.

   c.

   d.

PHILIPPIANS 1:1–11 — LESSON #2

3. Define the following words so that you will have a better understanding of Paul's meaning:

   a. Love (v. 9)

   b. Approve (v. 10)

   c. Sincere (v. 10)

   d. Righteousness (v. 11)

4. Paul's prayer for the church at Philippi was that their love would grow in knowledge and discernment, that they would approve the things that were excellent (be able to distinguish good from evil), be sincere in their demonstration of Christ, and be filled with the fruits of righteousness so that God would be glorified. How do we exhibit a sincere demonstration of Christ?

   a. Matthew 5:16

   b. Romans 12:9–11

   c. Philippians 2:14, 15

©2001—Morningstar Christian Chapel, Whittier, CA

PHILIPPIANS 1:1–11 **LESSON #2**

   d. Colossians 4:5, 6

   e. 1 Peter 2:12

5. In today's lesson, what *instructions* do we need to follow? What *warnings* must we heed? Are there any *promises* we can rest our faith upon?

6. Close your study time in prayer asking the Lord Jesus to make any necessary changes in your heart, mind and attitude this week!

DAY 6—BEGIN IN PRAYER

1. Read Philippians 1:1–11.

2. What lessons from this study have caused you to think, act, or speak differently?

3. How has the Lord specifically touched your heart this week? Will you surrender your life to His perfect will so that you will shine brightly and demonstrate the life of Christ more boldly today?

4. How are you doing on your memory verse for this week? *If you do not remember it yet, work on it today.*

Being confident of this very thing, that He which hath begun a good work in you will perform it until the day of Jesus Christ. Philippians 1:6

PHILIPPIANS 1:12–20 — LESSON #3

DAY 1—BEGIN IN PRAYER

1. Read Philippians 1.

2. Re-read Philippians 1:12–20.

3. What are the main topics in these verses?

4. Choose a verse to memorize this week. Begin working on it now.

DAY 2—BEGIN IN PRAYER

1. Read Philippians 1:12–13.

2. Beginning in Acts 21 and continuing through the end of the book of Acts we find the account of the *"things which had happened"* to Paul. The result of the persecution was a prison sentence of more than two years. What was the amazing outcome of his years in bondage, according to verse 12?

3. Paul had one supreme purpose in life and that was to spread the Gospel of Jesus Christ. He knew that no circumstance that touched his life was out of God's control and that everything he was allowed to face was according to God's perfect will. Paul saw the bondage of imprisonment as an opportunity to spread the Gospel. How do the following promises help you to turn the focus of your heart from any allowed bondage in your life, to seeing the circumstances as a new avenue of witness?

    a. Jeremiah 29:11

    b. Romans 8:28–30

overFLOWING joy

PHILIPPIANS 1:12-20 — LESSON #3

    c. 2Corinthians 4:15-18

4. Paul found himself imprisoned for the sake of the Gospel. However, this imprisonment allowed him to preach Jesus Christ among the palace guards and to Caesar's very household. He probably would never have had this opportunity any other way. It is true that we will face persecution for our faith as we seek to boldly share the Good News of the Lord Jesus Christ. What eternal truths do we learn from the following Scriptures about persecution?

    a. Matthew 5:10-12

    b. John 15:20

    c. 2Timothy 3:12

    d. 1Peter 2:19-21

5. In today's lesson, what *instructions* do we need to follow? What *warnings* must we heed? Are there any *promises* we can rest our faith upon?

6. Close your study time in prayer asking the Lord Jesus to make any necessary changes in your heart, mind and attitude this week!

| PHILIPPIANS 1:12–20 | 15 | LESSON #3 |

DAY 3—BEGIN IN PRAYER

1. Read Philippians 1:14–15.

2. Look up the definitions for the following words to get a deeper meaning of these verses.

   a. Brethren (v. 14)

   b. Bold (v. 14)

   c. Envy (v. 15)

   d. Strife (v. 15)

3. How will heeding the Lord's instructions and following the example of the disciples in the following references enable us to *"boldly speak the Word without fear"*?

   a. Acts 1:8

   b. Acts 4:13

   c. Acts 4:29

©2001—Morningstar Christian Chapel, Whittier, CA

d. Acts 4:31

4. To the apostle Paul the motivation of an individual was of no consequence. It mattered only that Christ was preached. There were some in his day who were preaching only to bring more hardship to his life. What do we learn about the ugly characteristics of *envy and strife* and how do we keep them from becoming a part of our lives?

   a. Romans 13:13, 14

   b. 1Corinthians 3:1-3

   c. Galatians 5:19-21

   d. James 3:14-16

   Personal: Are envy and strife making their home in your heart or mind? The good news is, with repentance comes immediate forgiveness and the power to rejoice when the Lord blesses others!

5. In today's lesson, what *instructions* do we need to follow? What *warnings* must we heed? Are there any *promises* we can rest our faith upon?

PHILIPPIANS 1:12–20 — LESSON #3

6. Close your study time in prayer asking the Lord Jesus to make any necessary changes in your heart, mind and attitude this week!

Day 4—Begin in Prayer

1. Read Philippians 1:16–18.

2. What brought joy and rejoicing to Paul's heart (v. 18)?

3. Paul declared that those who preached Christ out of a sincere love for the Lord knew that he was set for the defense of the Gospel. How do we become set for the defense of the gospel?

    a. 2Timothy 2:15

    b. 1Peter 3:15

    c. 1Thessalonians 2:4

4. Paul rejoiced that Christ was preached. It is our mission and calling to tell the world that salvation is to be found only in the Lord Jesus Christ, whose sacrifice on the cross at Calvary paid the price for our sins. What do these verses teach us about the preaching of the cross?

    a. 1Corinthians 1:18

©2001—Morningstar Christian Chapel, Whittier, CA

PHILIPPIANS 1:12–20   LESSON #3

b. 1Corinthians 1:23, 24

c. Galatians 6:14

The preaching of the cross is certain to bring a strong reaction from those who hear the truth of the Gospel. How does our Lord describe this for us in John 15:18–21?

5. In today's lesson, what *instructions* do we need to follow? What *warnings* must we heed? Are there any *promises* we can rest our faith upon?

6. Close your study time in prayer asking the Lord Jesus to make any necessary changes in your heart, mind and attitude this week!

Day 5—Begin in Prayer

1. Read Philippians 1:19–20.

2. Use your *Strong's Concordance, Vine's Dictionary,* or another resource you have available to you to define the following words.

   a. Prayer (v. 19)

   b. Magnified (v. 20)

PHILIPPIANS 1:12-20 — LESSON #3

3. Paul relied on the power of prayer to keep him in this hard time. He had no way of knowing whether the end result of his trial would lead to freedom or death. What more do we learn about prayer and the privilege we have been given to have intimate access to our Heavenly Father?

   a. Matthew 26:41

   b. Luke 18:1

   c. John 16:24

   d. Ephesians 6:18

   Personal: We have been given the awesome privilege of intercessory prayer. Are you in need of prayer or do you know someone who needs to be prayed for? Have you been faithful in prayer? Is there room for improvement? Lord, teach us to pray!

4. Paul trusted that God was in complete control of his life and that whatever the outcome, he desired only that Christ be magnified. How can we have this same confidence in the Sovereignty of God?

   a. Genesis 50:19-20

   b. 1 Samuel 2:1-10

c. Daniel 2:20-22

d. Romans 8:26-28

5. In today's lesson, what *instructions* do we need to follow? What *warnings* must we heed? Are there any *promises* we can rest our faith upon?

6. Close your study time in prayer asking the Lord Jesus to make any necessary changes in your heart, mind and attitude this week!

Day 6—Begin in Prayer

1. Read Philippians 1:12-20.

2. List a few of the lessons you've learned from this study.

3. How has the Lord moved you to change this week? Will you allow Him to change you?

PHILIPPIANS 1:12–20 — LESSON #3

4. Have you taken the opportunity to preach Christ this week? Ask the Lord to use you boldly.

5. How are you doing on your memory verse for this week? *If you do not remember it, work on it today.*

What then? Notwithstanding, every way, whether in pretense, or in truth, Christ is preached; and I therein do rejoice, yea, and will rejoice. Philippians 1:18

22

PHILIPPIANS 1:21–30 — LESSON #4

Day 1—Begin in Prayer

1. Read Philippians 1.

2. Re-read Philippians 1:21–30.

3. What are the main topics of these verses?

4. Choose a verse to memorize this week. Begin working on it now.

Day 2—Begin in Prayer

1. Read Philippians 1:21–23.

> "FOR PAUL, TO LIVE IS CHRIST, HIS LIFE IS WRAPPED UP IN CHRIST, IN WITNESSING OF CHRIST, IN FELLOWSHIP WITH CHRIST, IN THE GOAL TO MAKE HIS LIFE A CHANNEL THROUGH WHICH OTHERS MIGHT KNOW CHRIST."
> — John F. Walvoord "Philippians — Triumph in Christ"

2. The Lord must hold first place in our hearts and lives. What more can we learn about our need to realize that "to live **is** Christ"?

    a. John 11:25, 26

    b. Mark 12:30

Overflowing Joy

©2001—Morningstar Christian Chapel, Whittier, CA

PHILIPPIANS 1:21-30 LESSON #4

c. Galatians 2:20

d. Colossians 3:1-4

Personal: Verse 21 becomes a valuable test of our lives. Fill in the blanks as it applies to your life. "For me to live is _____ , but to die is _____ !"

Are there any changes that need to be made in your priorities? Allow the Lord to reveal His heart of love for you. This will cause you to become more single-minded and more able to declare with Paul, *"For to me to live is Christ..."*

3. Paul yearned to be with the Lord, yet he knew that if he remained on earth there would be much fruit from his labor. What do these verses tell us about "the fruit" that is the natural consequence of a life committed to the Lord Jesus Christ?

   a. Proverbs 11:30

   b. Matthew 7:16-20

   c. John 4:35-38

PHILIPPIANS 1:21–30

LESSON #4

d. Galatians 5:22–25

4. Define the following words.

   a. Gain (v. 21)

   b. Fruit (v. 22)

   c. Depart (v. 23)

5. In today's lesson, what *instructions* do we need to follow? What *warnings* must we heed? Are there any *promises* we can rest our faith upon?

6. Close your study time in prayer asking the Lord Jesus to make any necessary changes in your heart, mind and attitude this week!

DAY 3—BEGIN IN PRAYER

1. Read Philippians 1:24–26.

2. Why did Paul think it was better that he remained with them rather than going to be with the Lord, which was the longing and desire of his heart (vs. 25, 26)?

PHILIPPIANS 1:21-30 — LESSON #4

3. As believers, we are to be a source of strength, comfort, encouragement and guidance to one another just as Paul was to the church at Philippi. What do we learn from the following verses about this important "body ministry"?

   a. Romans 15:1-3

   b. Colossians 3:12-14

   c. Ephesians 4:32

   d. 1Thessalonians 5:14, 15

   e. 2Timothy 2:24-26

4. Read and meditate on 1Corinthians 12:18-27 and list your responsibilities as a member of the family of believers.

   Personal: How are you doing at being a strong, supportive member of the Body of Christ?

PHILIPPIANS 1:21–30 — LESSON #4

5. In today's lesson, what *instructions* do we need to follow? What *warnings* must we heed? Are there any *promises* we can rest our faith upon?

6. Close your study time in prayer asking the Lord Jesus to make any necessary changes in your heart, mind and attitude this week!

DAY 4—BEGIN IN PRAYER

1. Read Philippians 1:27–28.

2. Paul exhorts the church at Philippi to let their *conversation or conduct* be worthy of the gospel of Christ. What does he mean by this statement?

   As followers of the Lord Jesus Christ we declare that we believe what He teaches and have committed our lives to walking in His ways. According to the following verses, what characteristics must then be evident in our lives?

   a. Ephesians 4:1–3

   b. Philippians 2:1–4

   c. 1 Thessalonians 2:11–13

   d. 2 Peter 1:4-8

| PHILIPPIANS 1:21–30 | | LESSON #4 |

"YOU ARE WRITING A GOSPEL, A CHAPTER EACH DAY, BY THE DEEDS THAT YOU DO AND THE WORDS THAT YOU SAY. MEN READ WHAT YOU WRITE, WHETHER FAITHFUL OR TRUE. JUST WHAT IS THE GOSPEL ACCORDING TO YOU?" (SOURCE UNKNOWN)

3. One characteristic Paul is looking for among *(the Philippian)* believers is unity, a unity that would be spoken of throughout the land causing Paul to hear about it even before he came to see them. Record the Lord's direction to the church in John 13:34, 35.

Personal: How are you doing at creating unity in your family, neighborhood and church?

4. Paul cautions the believers not to be "terrified" by their adversaries. Use your Bible Dictionary or Concordance to find the definition of these words.

   a. Terrified (v. 28)

   b. Adversaries (v. 28)

   Why is there no need for us to be afraid of our enemies?

   a. Ephesians 6:10–13

   b. 1 John 4:4

c. 1 John 5:4

5. In today's lesson, what *instructions* do we need to follow? What *warnings* must we heed? Are there any *promises* we can rest our faith upon?

6. Close your study time in prayer asking the Lord Jesus to make any necessary changes in your heart, mind and attitude this week!

Day 5—Begin in Prayer

1. Read Philippians 1:29-30.

2. The encouragement we found in yesterday's lesson is that even though the enemy seeks our destruction we have no need to fear. In fact it is proof to us of our salvation. As Christians we have a calling that we cannot deny. According to verse 29, what certainty comes along with believing in the Lord Jesus Christ?

   Do you find any encouragement from the following verses regarding this promise of suffering in the life of the Christian?

   a. Acts 5:40-42

   b. Philippians 3:9-12

PHILIPPIANS 1:21–30   **LESSON #4**

c. 1Peter 2:20, 21

3. What is God's promise to those who are suffering persecution and hardship in this world for His sake?

   a. Matthew 5:10–12

   b. Romans 8:17

   c. 2Timothy 2:11, 12a

   d. 1Peter 5:10

4. The suffering is for *"His sake."* It is a privilege, a gift, and an honor! How can our suffering and victory in times of trial be an encouragement to others and the world?

   a. Matthew 5:14–16

   b. 2Corinthians 1:4, 5

PHILIPPIANS 1:21–30   LESSON #4

c. 1 Peter 4:14–16

5. In today's lesson, what *instructions* do we need to follow? What *warnings* must we heed? Are there any *promises* we can rest our faith upon?

6. Close your study time in prayer asking the Lord Jesus to make any necessary changes in your heart, mind and attitude this week!

DAY 6—BEGIN IN PRAYER

1. Read Philippians 1:21–30.

2. Make a list the main lessons you've learned this week.

3. How has the Lord touched your heart and caused you to draw closer to Him this week?

4. How are you doing on your memory verse for this week? *If you do not know it well yet, work on it today.*

For to me to live is Christ, and to die is gain. Philippians 1:21

32

PHILIPPIANS 2:1–11 — LESSON #5

DAY 1—BEGIN IN PRAYER

1. Read Philippians 2.

2. Re-read Philippians 2:1–11.

3. What are the main topics in these verses?

4. Choose a verse to memorize this week. Begin working on it now.

DAY 2—BEGIN IN PRAYER

1. Read Philippians 2:1–2.

2. What spiritual characteristic in the church would fulfill Paul's joy?

   List the four phrases he uses for this characteristic. (v. 2)

   a.

   b.

   c.

   d.

PHILIPPIANS 2:1-11 — LESSON #5

3. On what basis is Paul calling for this unity (v. 1)?

The characteristic of unity, which Paul pleaded for and the Scriptures require, often eludes the church because pride and selfishness have taken hold of the hearts of men. Use the following Scriptures as exhortation and encouragement to walk in the unity that is ours through Christ Jesus our Lord.

a. Psalm 133:1

b. John 17:20-23

c. Romans 15:5, 6

d. 1Corinthians 1:10-13

e. 2Corinthians 13:11

f. 1Peter 3:8, 9

4. Unity is different from uniformity. Explain the difference from your experience.

PHILIPPIANS 2:1–11 — LESSON #5

5. In today's lesson, what *instructions* do we need to follow? What *warnings* must we heed? Are there any *promises* we can rest our faith upon?

6. Close your study time in prayer asking the Lord Jesus to make any necessary changes in your heart, mind and attitude this week!

DAY 3—BEGIN IN PRAYER

1. Read Philippians 2:3–4.

2. The root problem behind discord is pride. Unity begins with humility and Paul gives us a picture of how a humble person conducts himself. What four phrases in verses 3 and 4 give us a necessary pattern to follow?

    a.

    b.

    c.

    d.

3. The truly humble person is concerned with the needs and cares of others. He willingly yields himself to Christ to be a servant, to use what he is and has for the glory of God and the good of those he comes in contact with.

©2001—MORNINGSTAR CHRISTIAN CHAPEL, WHITTIER, CA

PHILIPPIANS 2:1–11 — LESSON #5

What do these verses teach us about humility?

a. Isaiah 66:1, 2

b. Romans 12:10

c. Ephesians 4:1–3

d. 1 Peter 5:5, 6

4. Pride is the opposite of submission. God's Word is clear about His attitude toward pride. What warnings are given in these verses about pride and how do they assist you in surrendering your life fully to the Lord today?

a. Proverbs 8:13

b. Proverbs 6:16–19

c. Mark 7:20–23

d. 1 John 2:16

PHILIPPIANS 2:1–11 — LESSON #5

5. In today's lesson, what *instructions* do we need to follow? What *warnings* must we heed? Are there any *promises* we can rest our faith upon?

6. Close your study time in prayer asking the Lord Jesus to make any necessary changes in your heart, mind and attitude this week!

DAY 4—BEGIN IN PRAYER

1. Read Philippians 2:5–8.

2. Paul gives us the ultimate example of humility. God, taking on the form of a servant, humbled Himself and died in our place. What more do these verses teach us about true humility?

   a. Isaiah 53 (Note a few phrases that best illustrate the Lord's true humility.)

   b. Romans 15:1–5

   c. Hebrews 12:1–3

   d. 1 Peter 2:21–25

3. Look up the definition of the following words for a better understanding of this key quality of humility that is essential in the life of every true Christian.

   a. Mind (v. 5)

PHILIPPIANS 2:1-11 — LESSON #5

b. No reputation (v. 7)

c. Servant (v. 7)

d. Humbled (v. 8)

4. Paul exhorts us to, *"Let this mind be in you which was also in Christ Jesus."* We are called to humility and submission because we are to live our lives as our Savior did.

"OUR THINKING, OUR ATTITUDE, OUR OPINION, OUR EVALUATION OF THE SITUATION WHICH FACES US SHOULD BE THE SAME AS CHRIST'S WHEN HE FACED HIS SUPREME ACT OF HUMILIATION AND DEATH." JOHN WALVOORD—PHILIPPIANS

All the above being true, what direction are we given to follow in Colossians 3:12-17 regarding our relationships with one another?

5. In today's lesson, what *instructions* do we need to follow? What *warnings* must we heed? Are there any *promises* we can rest our faith upon?

6. Close your study time in prayer asking the Lord Jesus to make any necessary changes in your heart, mind and attitude this week!

©2001—MORNINGSTAR CHRISTIAN CHAPEL, WHITTIER, CA

| PHILIPPIANS 2:1-11 | 39 | LESSON #5 |

DAY 5—BEGIN IN PRAYER

1. Read Philippians 2:9-11.

   The outcome of humility in Jesus' life was His exaltation and the glory of the Father.

   "THE EXALTATION WHICH CHRIST EXPERIENCED WHEN HE WENT TO HEAVEN WAS NOT ONLY THE RESUMPTION OF THE GLORY WHICH HE HAD BEFORE THE INCARNATION (JOHN 17:5), BUT THE ADDED GLORY OF TRIUMPH OVER SIN, SUFFERING AND DEATH, AND THE FULFILLMENT OF GOD THAT IN HIS DEATH HE WOULD RECONCILE THE WORLD UNTO HIMSELF. (2CORINTHIANS 5:19)" JOHN WALVOORD

2. What do these scriptures teach us about the exaltation of the Lord Jesus Christ?

   a. Daniel 7:13-14

   b. Revelation 1:5, 6

   c. Revelation 5:11-13

3. It is written that, *"Every knee **shall bow** and **every tongue shall confess** that Jesus Christ is Lord."* When will this take place?

   a. Romans 14:10-12

©2001—MORNINGSTAR CHRISTIAN CHAPEL, WHITTIER, CA

PHILIPPIANS 2:1–11 — LESSON #5

b. John 5:25–29

c. Revelation 20:11, 12

4. The life of humility that Jesus lived, thinking of others, serving others, and sacrificing for others, brought glory to God the Father. As Christians, our lives of humility and submission also glorify God. How will the following verses help you to walk more sacrificially today?

a. Isaiah 57:15

b. Matthew 5:3

c. 1 Peter 5:6, 7

d. James 4:7–10

5. In today's lesson, what *instructions* do we need to follow? What *warnings* must we heed? Are there any *promises* we can rest our faith upon?

6. Close your study time in prayer asking the Lord Jesus to make any necessary changes in your heart, mind and attitude this week!

PHILIPPIANS 2:1–11 — LESSON #5

DAY 6—BEGIN IN PRAYER

1. Read Philippians 2:1–11.

2. Make a list of the main lessons you've learned regarding the characteristics of unity, humility and pride.

3. In what areas has the Lord spoken to you? Pray, humbling yourself before Him, asking Him to change your heart and life.

4. How are you doing on your memory verse for this week? *If you do not remember it yet, work on it today.*

Let this mind be in you, which was also in Christ Jesus: Philippians 2:5

42

PHILIPPIANS 2:12–18 — LESSON #6

DAY 1—BEGIN IN PRAYER

1. Read Philippians 2.

2. Re-read Philippians 2:12–18.

3. What are the main topics of these verses?

4. Choose a verse to memorize this week. Begin working on it now.

DAY 2—BEGIN IN PRAYER

1. Read Philippians 2:12–13.

2. Look up the definitions for the following words.

    a. Beloved (v. 12)

    b. Obeyed (v. 12)

    c. Good Pleasure (v. 13)

3. In verse 12, Paul is not saying we must work "for" our salvation, or "toward" our salvation, or "at" our salvation. He says we must work "out" our salvation. No one can work out his salvation unless God has already worked it in.

overFLOWING joy

©2001—Morningstar Christian Chapel, Whittier, CA

PHILIPPIANS 2:12-18 — LESSON #6

"IT TEACHES THAT BECAUSE YOU ARE ALREADY SAVED, BECAUSE GOD HAS ALREADY ENTERED YOUR LIFE IN THE PERSON OF THE HOLY SPIRIT, BECAUSE YOU, THEREFORE, HAVE HIS POWER AT WORK WITHIN YOU—BECAUSE OF THESE THINGS YOU ARE NOW TO STRIVE TO EXPRESS THIS SALVATION IN YOUR CONDUCT." BOICE—PHILIPPIANS

How do the following verses teach us more about how our salvation is to affect our daily conduct and the discipline with which we are to work *out our salvation?*

a. 2Peter 1:5-10

b. Romans 13:11-14

c. 1Corinthians 9:24-27

d. 1Corinthians 15:58

4. The good news is God does not expect us to accomplish this work on our own. It is His Spirit in us that enables us to "desire" and to "accomplish" His good pleasure. How do the following Scriptures encourage you about His working in your life?

a. Ezekiel 36:26, 27

b. 2Corinthians 3:18

©2001—MORNINGSTAR CHRISTIAN CHAPEL, WHITTIER, CA

PHILIPPIANS 2:12-18 — LESSON #6

c. Ephesians 2:10

d. Hebrews 13:20, 21

5. In today's lesson, what *instructions* do we need to follow? What *warnings* must we heed? Are there any *promises* we can rest our faith upon?

6. Close your study time in prayer asking the Lord Jesus to make any necessary changes in your heart, mind and attitude this week!

Day 3—Begin in Prayer

1. Read Philippians 2:14-15.

2. The word *"without"* suggests isolation, so Paul was saying that the believer is to be isolated from murmurings and disputings. Murmuring is the outcome of a discontented soul. In contrast to the ways of the world, we ought to be walking in peace and contentment. Our service and our every action are to be *"as unto the Lord."* What do these verses teach us about the correct motivation for all that we say and do?

a. Ephesians 6:5-7

b. Colossians 3:22, 23

PHILIPPIANS 2:12-18 — LESSON #6

c. Galatians 1:10

d. 1 Peter 2:13-15

Personal: We need to be very careful that our lives do not become over run by this negative characteristic of murmuring and disputing! Do you have a contented heart that will keep you from complaining and fighting? If not, stop now and confess this sin to the Lord asking Him to remind you of all that He has done on your behalf and of every blessing that is yours because you are His child.

3. Use your Dictionary of New Testament Words or Concordance to define the following words.

   a. Murmuring (Complaining—NKJV) (v. 14)

   b. Disputing (v. 14)

   c. Blameless (v. 15)

   d. Harmless (v. 15)

4. The outcome of God's working in us is that our lifestyle will be obviously opposite from those who are of the *"crooked and perverse nation."* The work of the Holy Spirit in our lives will cause us to shine brightly and allow us to be a powerful example to the world. Use the following references as a reminder of the ministry we have been given to those who do not yet know the Lord Jesus Christ.

   a. Proverbs 4:18

   b. Matthew 5:14-16

   c. Titus 2:9, 10

   d. 1Peter 2:12

5. In today's lesson, what *instructions* do we need to follow? What *warnings* must we heed? Are there any *promises* we can rest our faith upon?

6. Close your study time in prayer asking the Lord Jesus to make any necessary changes in your heart, mind and attitude this week!

DAY 4 ~ BEGIN IN PRAYER

1. Read Philippians 2:16.

PHILIPPIANS 2:12-18 — LESSON #6

2. Paul's exhortation to the Philippians, and to us, *"to hold forth the Word of Life"* gives us a clear example of the saving power of the Word. What truths must be made perfectly clear if we are to lead others to life in Christ?

   a. Romans 3:23

   b. Romans 5:8

   c. Romans 6:23

   d. Romans 10:13

   e. Romans 10:9, 10

3. The Bible is God's love letter to His children. It is life and truth, guidance and comfort, correction and reproof. It has the answer to every problem and the direction for every situation. What do we learn from these verses about the Word of God?

   a. Psalm 119:130

   b. Romans 1:16

PHILIPPIANS 2:12–18 — LESSON #6

c. Hebrews 4:12, 13

d. 2Timothy 3:16, 17

Personal: In Job 23:12, Job says, "Neither have I gone back from the commandment of His lips; I have esteemed the words of His mouth more than my necessary food." Do you have this love for the Word? Are you spending time daily studying, reading, and listening to God speak to you through His Word? Do you esteem His Word more than your necessary food? This is the basis for a victorious Christian life.

4. Paul's desire was that those who trusted in the Word of the Lord would endure to the end so that his labor would not have been in vain. Look up the following verses and as you meditate on them ask the Lord to deepen your love for His Word so that you will be firmly grounded in the Word of Life.

    a. Psalm 19:9, 10

    b. Psalm 119:11

    c. Jeremiah 15:16

5. In today's lesson, what *instructions* do we need to follow? What *warnings* must we heed? Are there any *promises* we can rest our faith upon?

©2001—Morningstar Christian Chapel, Whittier, CA

PHILIPPIANS 2:12-18 — LESSON #6

6. Close your study time in prayer asking the Lord Jesus to make any necessary changes in your heart, mind and attitude this week!

DAY 5—BEGIN IN PRAYER

1. Read Philippians 2:17-18.

2. Paul uses his life as an example of submission and humility. He declares, *"I am poured out as a drink offering on the sacrifice and service of your faith."* He willingly sacrificed his life on their behalf. What do these verses tell us about our need to humbly submit our lives to the Lord, trusting His perfect plan, and being willing to sacrifice our lives for others?

   a. John 15:12, 13

   b. Ephesians 5:1, 2

   c. 2Timothy 2:8-10

   d. 1John 3:14-17

3. Record the definitions for the following words and consider how their meaning can affect your walk with the Lord today.

   a. Offered (v. 17)

©2001—MORNINGSTAR CHRISTIAN CHAPEL, WHITTIER, CA

PHILIPPIANS 2:12–18 — LESSON #6

b. Service (v. 17)

c. Faith (v. 17)

d. Rejoice (v. 17)

4. Paul calls for mutual celebration over God's work in the midst of the church at Philippi. He was placing his own achievements, even his own martyrdom, at a very low point in comparison to the value of their strong, enduring faith in Christ. What more can we learn about a faith that endures until the end?

   a. Matthew 24:13

   b. Hebrews 3:14

   c. James 5:7, 8

   d. Revelation 2:10

5. In today's lesson, what *instructions* do we need to follow? What *warnings* must we heed? Are there any *promises* we can rest our faith upon?

©2001—Morningstar Christian Chapel, Whittier, CA

PHILIPPIANS 2:12–18 — LESSON #6

6. Close your study time in prayer asking the Lord Jesus to make any necessary changes in your heart, mind and attitude this week!

DAY 6—BEGIN IN PRAYER

1. Read Philippians 2:12–18.

2. List the lessons you've learned this week.

3. In what area has the Lord spoken to you this week? How has He called you to change? Spend some time in prayer, asking Him to do this work in you. He is waiting for you to call on Him!

4. How are you doing on your memory verse for this week? *If you do not remember it, work on it today.*

For it is God which worketh in you both to will and to do of His good pleasure. Philippians 2:13

PHILIPPIANS 2:19–30 — LESSON #7

Day 1—Begin in Prayer

1. Read Philippians 2.

2. Re-read Philippians 2:19–30.

3. What are the main topics of these verses?

4. Choose a verse to memorize this week. Begin working on it now.

Day 2—Begin in Prayer

1. Read Philippians 2:19–21.

2. Paul hoped to send Timothy to represent him to the church at Philippi. In his description of the character of this young man we find a vivid example of what the Christian life should be. How does Paul describe Timothy?

   Look up the following verses to learn more about Timothy. Record the facts you discover.

   a. Acts 16:1–3

   b. Acts 19:21, 22

   c. 1 Corinthians 4:15–17

d. 1 Thessalonians 3:2

e. 1 Timothy 1:1, 2a

3. The ministry of the church and the responsibility of every believer is to spread the good news of the Lord Jesus Christ. This cannot be accomplished effectively when only a few choose to serve while the majority seek to be served. This was a problem in Rome where Paul was imprisoned and is often a problem in the modern church. According to the following verses what type of commitment is required of the Christian?

   a. Mark 12:29-31

   b. Luke 9:23-25

   c. Luke 9:59-62

4. What more can we learn from the following Scriptures regarding the very necessary characteristic of every true believer - servanthood?

   a. Matthew 25:23

   b. Mark 9:35

PHILIPPIANS 2:19–30 — LESSON #7

c. Luke 16:13

d. John 15:20

5. In today's lesson, what *instructions* do we need to follow? What *warnings* must we heed? Are there any *promises* we can rest our faith upon?

6. Close your study time in prayer asking the Lord Jesus to make any necessary changes in your heart, mind and attitude this week!

DAY 3—BEGIN IN PRAYER

1. Read Philippians 2:22–24.

2. In verse 22, Paul states, *"you know the proof of Him,"* or you know his proven character. Timothy had established a reputation as a servant. Paul lays before us Timothy's life as an example of humility. What do the following verses tell us about what our reputation must be with others?

   a. 1 Timothy 3:7

   b. 1 Thessalonians 5:22

   c. Titus 2:1–8

©2001—MORNINGSTAR CHRISTIAN CHAPEL, WHITTIER, CA

d. 1 Corinthians 10:31-33

3. Read Philippians 2:22 carefully. What phrase speaks of Timothy's ability to be a team worker?

According to 1 Corinthians 12:12-27, how are we to work together to be the faithful witnesses that the Lord desires?

Personal: How are you doing at being a faithful team worker? Would those in your family and your church speak as highly of you as Paul did of Timothy?

4. Paul was willing to send one of his *only* helpers to Philippi with the news of the trial results, and to comfort and encourage them. Look up the following verses about *sacrificial love — Agape*. What example is there for us to follow?

a. John 15:13

b. Ephesians 5:2

c. 1 John 4:7-11

PHILIPPIANS 2:19–30 — LESSON #7

d. 1 Peter 4:8

5. In today's lesson, what *instructions* do we need to follow? What *warnings* must we heed? Are there any *promises* we can rest our faith upon?

6. Close your study time in prayer asking the Lord Jesus to make any necessary changes in your heart, mind and attitude this week!

Day 4—Begin in Prayer

1. Read Philippians 2:25–27.

2. In these verses Paul introduces another faithful servant. He had nothing but praise for this otherwise unknown Christian. What four descriptive terms does he use to describe Epaphroditus?

    a.

    b.

    c.

    d.

PHILIPPIANS 2:19–30 — LESSON #7

Paul called Epaphroditus his *"fellow soldier."* With this terminology we are given the picture of the spiritual battle we face as believers. How do the following references add to this picture and encourage you to be ready for the warfare you will face today?

a. 2 Corinthians 10:3–5

b. Ephesians 6:11–13

c. 1 Timothy 6:11, 12

d. 2 Timothy 2:3, 4

e. 1 Peter 5:8, 9

3. Epaphroditus risked his very life to serve the Lord by ministering to the needs of Paul. We are told that he was *"full of heaviness"* — *"ademoneo"* in Greek. This is the strongest of three Greek words for depression. Interestingly, why was he suffering such grave depression (v. 26)?

According to the Psalmist, what is the primary answer for depression in our lives? See Psalm 43:5.

©2001—Morningstar Christian Chapel, Whittier, CA

PHILIPPIANS 2:19–30 — LESSON #7

4. Epaphroditus recovered from his desperate illness and Paul saw in his restoration another token of the mercy of God. God saved this servant's life and Paul was spared the added sorrow of losing the fellowship of a spiritual brother who risked his life to serve him. What reminder of God's ever present mercy in our lives do you find as you read and meditate on Psalm 136? Record the main point of this Psalm.

5. In today's lesson, what *instructions* do we need to follow? What *warnings* must we heed? Are there any *promises* we can rest our faith upon?

6. Close your study time in prayer asking the Lord Jesus to make any necessary changes in your heart, mind and attitude this week!

Day 5—Begin in Prayer

1. Read Philippians 2:28–30.

2. Paul had developed a very close relationship with those who served with him in the ministry of the gospel. What are the benefits of this kind of support?

   a. Ecclesiastes 4:9, 10

   b. Proverbs 17:17a

   c. Proverbs 27:17

PHILIPPIANS 2:19–30   **LESSON #7**

3. Paul instructed the Philippians to receive Epaphroditus with all gladness and hold him in high esteem. What do these verses say about our need to encourage and value one another?

   a. John 15:12

   b. Romans 15:1–3

   c. Galatians 6:1, 2

   d. Philippians 2:3

   e. 1 Thessalonians 5: 14, 15

4. Look up the definition of the following words.

   a. Receive (v. 29)

   b. Gladness (v. 29)

   c. Reputation (esteem—NKJV) (v. 29)

Philippians 2:19–30   Lesson #7

5. In today's lesson, what *instructions* do we need to follow? What *warnings* must we heed? Are there any *promises* we can rest our faith upon?

6. Close your study time in prayer asking the Lord Jesus to make any necessary changes in your heart, mind and attitude this week!

Day 6—Begin in Prayer

1. Read Philippians 2:19–30.

2. List the lessons you've learned from your study of Philippians this week.

3. How has the Lord encouraged you to increase in love? To die to yourself? To love His Word? Ask in prayer that He would continue the work in you today.

4. How are you doing on your memory verse for this week? *If you do not remember it, work on it today.*

For I have no man likeminded, who will naturally care for your state.
Philippians 2:20

PHILIPPIANS 3:1–11   LESSON #8

Day 1—Begin in Prayer

1. Read Philippians 3.

2. Re-read Philippians 3:1–11.

3. What are the main topics in these verses?

4. Choose a verse to memorize this week. Begin working on it now.

Day 2—Begin in Prayer

1. Read Philippians 3:1–3.

2. Paul begins Chapter 3 with a challenge to the believers to rejoice *in the Lord*. It would be seemingly impossible if we were to rejoice *in* our circumstances, *in* our trials, or *in* our hardships. However, is it possible to rejoice in the Lord in spite of the circumstances?

   As a Christian, what reasons do you have to rejoice *in the Lord* every minute of everyday?

   What encouragement and reminder do we find in these verses about the reasons that our hearts ought to be filled with rejoicing?

   a. Psalm 5:11

Philippians 3:1-11 — Lesson #8

b. Isaiah 61:10, 11

c. 2Timothy 1:8, 9

d. 1Peter 2:9, 10

3. Just as today, there were many in Paul's day who taught false doctrines. Paul warns this young church (and us) to beware of those who would seek to destroy them by leading them away from the truth of God's Word. These verses suggest that joy be founded, to a very large degree, on sound doctrine. How do the following verses support the fact that our joy comes from trusting the unchanging truth of God's Word?

   a. Jeremiah 15:16

   b. Psalm 19:8-11

   c. Psalm 119:14-16

   d. John 15:10, 11

4. Use your dictionary of New Testament Words to define the following words so that you may have better understanding of Paul's warning.

PHILIPPIANS 3:1–11 — LESSON #8

a. Beware (v. 2)

b. Evil worker (v. 2)

c. Rejoice (v. 3)

d. Confidence *(no)* (v. 3)

5. In today's lesson, what *instructions* do we need to follow? What *warnings* must we heed? Are there any *promises* we can rest our faith upon?

6. Close your study time in prayer asking the Lord Jesus to make any necessary changes in your heart, mind and attitude this week!

DAY 3—BEGIN IN PRAYER

1. Read Philippians 3:4–7.

2. If anyone could boast of his religious achievements, Paul says, "I could have." However, when he came face-to-face with the true righteousness of Christ he counted all as nothing. What do we learn about man's righteousness from the following verses?

a. Isaiah 64:6

b. Job 15:14

c. Romans 7:18-20

3. Read Acts 9:1-31. List the events of Paul's conversion.

4. What was Paul's attitude about his "righteousness" after meeting the Lord? See Philippians 3:7.

If we are to *boast* in anything, Who or what is it to be?

a. Jeremiah 9:23, 24

b. 1 Corinthians 1:27-31

c. 1 Corinthians 4:7

d. Galatians 6:14

| PHILIPPIANS 3:1-11 | | LESSON #8 |

"HE IS NO FOOL TO GIVE UP WHAT HE CANNOT KEEP TO GAIN WHAT HE CANNOT LOSE." JIM ELLIOT

5. In today's lesson, what *instructions* do we need to follow? What *warnings* must we heed? Are there any *promises* we can rest our faith upon?

6. Close your study time in prayer asking the Lord Jesus to make any necessary changes in your heart, mind and attitude this week!

DAY 4—BEGIN IN PRAYER

1. Read Philippians 3:8-9.

2. Paul said he *"counted all things but loss for the excellency of the knowledge of Christ Jesus."* In fact he compared all those things to animal waste. He had given up everything for Christ and he did so without regret. He had seen his Lord and Savior face-to-face and he willingly set aside his home, his position in the Sanhedrin, the favor of his community, his health and even the acceptance of the Jerusalem church to serve the Lord Jesus Christ. He would later give his life on the altar of Nero's hate. What do these verses teach us about the law, which Paul had previously depended upon?

   a. Acts 13:38, 39

   b. Galatians 2:16

   c. Galatians 3:24, 25

©2001—MORNINGSTAR CHRISTIAN CHAPEL, WHITTIER, CA

3. Salvation is largely a matter of one's position. The unsaved man is without Christ, without God, without hope. The saved man is "Found in Him." How do we obtain true spiritual righteousness (v. 9)?

What more do we learn about true righteousness from Romans 3:21-25?

4. How do the following Scriptures help you to establish the **right** attitude toward the things of this world?

   a. Matthew 6:19-21

   b. Luke 12:16-21

   c. 1 Timothy 6:17-19

   d. Hebrews 13:5

5. In today's lesson, what *instructions* do we need to follow? What *warnings* must we heed? Are there any *promises* we can rest our faith upon?

6. Close your study time in prayer asking the Lord Jesus to make any necessary changes in your heart, mind and attitude this week!

| PHILIPPIANS 3:1–11 | 69 | LESSON #8 |

DAY 5—BEGIN IN PRAYER

1. Read Philippians 3:10–11.

2. In verse 10, what four phrases describe Paul's spiritual goal for himself, and the goal we need to seek after if we desire to be conformed more into the likeness of our Lord and Savior?

   a.

   b.

   c.

   d.

3. The word *"know"* in verse 10 means: *to know experientially.* It describes a relationship by personal experience. We are to know Christ intimately, to have a personal relationship, daily communion and fellowship with Him, and a constantly deepening commitment to Him. We need to *"know"* Him with our hearts, not simply with our minds. What do the following verses teach us about our intimate relationship with the Lord and how it will be made manifest to the world?

   a. Deuteronomy 6:5–7

   b. Psalm 40:8–10

PHILIPPIANS 3:1–11 — LESSON #8

c. John 14:21

d. 1 John 2:5, 6

4. We need the power of the resurrection to enable us to live obedient lives in Christ. Our obedience will bring us suffering in the form of persecution from those who hate Christ. As we draw closer to the Lord, we become more like Him and more like who we will be at the resurrection. What do we learn about this process of spiritual growth that is taking place in each of our lives?

   a. 2 Corinthians 3:18

   b. Colossians 3:8–10

   c. Romans 8:28–30

   d. 1 John 3:1–3

5. In today's lesson, what *instructions* do we need to follow? What *warnings* must we heed? Are there any *promises* we can rest our faith upon?

6. Close your study time in prayer asking the Lord Jesus to make any necessary changes in your heart, mind and attitude this week!

PHILIPPIANS 3:1–11 — LESSON #8

DAY 6—BEGIN IN PRAYER

1. Read Philippians 3:1–11.

2. List the lessons you've learned this week.

3. How has the Lord spoken to you this week? What do you count as *"loss for the excellency of the knowledge of Christ"*? Allow the Lord to work His will in your heart today!

4. How are you doing on your memory verse for this week? *If you do not remember it, work on it today.*

> *Yea doubtless, and I count all things but loss for the excellency of the knowledge of Christ Jesus my Lord: for whom I have suffered the loss of all things, and do count them but dung, that I may win Christ... Philippians 3:8*

72

PHILIPPIANS 3:12–21 — LESSON #9

DAY 1—BEGIN IN PRAYER

1. Read Philippians 3.

2. Re-read Philippians 3:12–21.

3. What are the main topics in these verses?

4. Choose a verse to memorize this week. Begin working on it now.

DAY 2—BEGIN IN PRAYER

1. Read Philippians 3:12–14.

2. Paul gives us the illustration of an athlete striving to win the prize. He teaches us that we are to strive to reach the goal of maturity in Christ. In verse 12 he declares, *"Not as though I have already attained..."* What do we learn about our need to diligently run this race?

   a. 1 Corinthians 9:24, 25

   b. 1 Timothy 6:11, 12

   c. Hebrews 12:1, 2

PHILIPPIANS 3:12-21   74   LESSON #9

3. In order to run to win, our eyes must be on the future, not the past. To "forget" in this verse means to no longer be influenced by or affected by. What does God's Word say about those things of the past and how we should view them?

   a. John 5:24

   b. Romans 5:1, 2

   c. Romans 8:1, 2

   d. 2Corinthians 5:17

4. Paul declares that with all his ability he is *"Pressing toward the mark for the prize of the high calling of God in Christ Jesus."* We have been "called" by God and this calling brings with it the responsibility of doing the very best we can, by the power of the Holy Spirit, to press forward in Christ. What do we learn about our calling and our responsibility to respond appropriately to it?

   a. Romans 12:1, 2

   b. Ephesians 4:1-3

   c. 1Thessalonians 2:11-13

PHILIPPIANS 3:12-21 — LESSON #9

d. 1 Peter 5:8-10

5. In today's lesson, what *instructions* do we need to follow? What *warnings* must we heed? Are there any *promises* we can rest our faith upon?

6. Close your study time in prayer asking the Lord Jesus to make any necessary changes in your heart, mind and attitude this week!

DAY 3—BEGIN IN PRAYER

1. Read Philippians 3:15-16.

2. Paul is calling for those who are mature, or are striving toward maturity, to have the same mind, the same mind set and attitude that he had toward the Lord and toward the world. Remember what he states in verses 13 and 14, *"This one thing I do...press toward the mark of the high calling of God in Christ Jesus."* In order to achieve this goal we must be single-minded. What does the Bible say about those who are **not** single-minded?

    a. Isaiah 29:13

    b. Matthew 6:22-24

    c. James 1:8

©2001—MORNINGSTAR CHRISTIAN CHAPEL, WHITTIER, CA

PHILIPPIANS 3:12–21 — LESSON #9

d. James 4:8

3. It is not enough to run hard and win the race; the runner must also obey **all** the rules. In verses 15 and 16, Paul emphasizes the importance of the Christian remembering the "spiritual rules" laid down in the Word of God. Many followed Paul's unhindered commitment, but there were some who were *otherwise minded*. He committed those to the mighty hand of God. What do we learn about our obligation, as Christians, to be obedient to God's commands?

   a. Luke 6:46–49

   b. John 15:12–14

   c. 2Timothy 2:3–5

   d. 1John 2:3–7

4. Define the following words to give you a clearer understanding of these verses.

   a. Perfect (NKJV—Mature) (v. 15)

   b. Minded (NKJV—have this mind) (v. 15)

   c. Attained (v. 16)

d. Walk (v. 16)

5. In today's lesson, what *instructions* do we need to follow? What *warnings* must we heed? Are there any *promises* we can rest our faith upon?

6. Close your study time in prayer asking the Lord Jesus to make any necessary changes in your heart, mind and attitude this week!

Day 4—Begin in Prayer

1. Read Philippians 3:17-19.

2. Paul was able to say to the Philippians, *"...be followers together of me..."* He offered his life as an example for them to follow in their pursuit of Christ. How are our lives to be lived so that others should follow?

   a. 1 Timothy 4:12, 13

   b. 2 Timothy 2:22-26

   c. Titus 2:7, 8

   d. James 3:13

3. Paul warned the church at Philippi (and he is warning us) to beware that there will come in among them those who are sworn enemies of the cross.

Sadly, they often come in disguise. We are to be wise in hearing and careful to discern the truth when we listen to the teaching of the Word. How do these verses help to remind us of our responsibility to discern the truth about what we hear?

a. Proverbs 2:1–5

b. Acts 17:10, 11

c. 2Timothy 3:15, 16

4. Paul's heart broke for those who were his enemies (v. 18) and he was aware of their end—eternal separation from the Lord (v. 19). He found no consolation in this knowledge, in spite of all the damage they had done to him and to his fellow believers. What do the following verses teach us about our relationship to our enemies?

a. Matthew 5:43, 44

b. Luke 6:27–31

c. Romans 12:19–21

d. 1Peter 3:8, 9

PHILIPPIANS 3:12–21 — LESSON #9

Personal: Is your heart breaking over the eternal destiny of your enemies? Have you shed tears for them? Ask the Lord to soften your heart and allow you to see them as He does, in agape love!

5. In today's lesson, what *instructions* do we need to follow? What *warnings* must we heed? Are there any *promises* we can rest our faith upon?

6. Close your study time in prayer asking the Lord Jesus to make any necessary changes in your heart, mind and attitude this week!

DAY 5—BEGIN IN PRAYER

1. Read Philippians 3:20–21.

2. We are, as believers, citizens of another country. We are to have a completely different view of the world than the unbeliever. Right now we are pilgrims and strangers in a foreign land. With each day that we live, we pitch our tents just that much closer to the place where we have our true citizenship. What more do we learn about our citizenship from the following verses?

   a. 2Corinthians 4:18; 5:1

   b. Hebrews 11:9, 10 and 13–16

   c. Colossians 3:1–3

PHILIPPIANS 3:12-21 — LESSON #9

3. Our citizenship is in heaven and the King of that country is coming back to earth. He is coming to receive His bride to Himself. She is to be waiting expectantly. Our view of, and reaction to, the circumstances we face, the trials we must endure and the hardships we bear must be that of one who looks intently for the coming of his Savior. How are we to live in light of His soon return?

   a. Mark 13:33-37

   b. 1 Corinthians 16:13

   c. 1 Thessalonians 5:1-6

   d. 1 Peter 4:7, 8

   > Jesus said, "...I go to prepare a place for you. And if I go and prepare a place for you, I will come again, and receive you unto myself; that where I am, there ye may be also." John 14:2, 3
   > **(Perhaps Today!)**

4. At the resurrection we shall receive a new body, one fit for eternity. What do we learn from the following Scriptures regarding this wonderful, much anticipated change?

   a. 1 Corinthians 15:42-44

PHILIPPIANS 3:12–21   LESSON #9

    b. 1 Corinthians 15:48–54

    c. 1 Thessalonians 4:14–17

5. In today's lesson, what *instructions* do we need to follow? What *warnings* must we heed? Are there any *promises* we can rest our faith upon?

6. Close your study time in prayer asking the Lord Jesus to make any necessary changes in your heart, mind and attitude this week!

DAY 6—BEGIN IN PRAYER

1. Read Philippians 3:12–21.

2. List the lessons you've learned this week.

3. Are you pressing toward the mark? Are you heavenly minded? Are you looking for the soon return of the Lord? Spend time in prayer asking the Lord to make any needed changes in your words, attitudes or actions.

4. How are you doing on your memory verse for this week? *If you do not remember it, work on it today.*

Brethren, I count not myself to have apprehended: but this one thing I do, forgetting those things which are behind, and reaching forth unto those things which are before, I press toward the mark for the prize of the high calling of God in Christ Jesus. Philippians 3:13, 14

PHILIPPIANS 4:1–9 — LESSON #10

DAY 1—BEGIN IN PRAYER

1. Read Philippians 4.

2. Re-read Philippians 4:1–9.

3. What are the main topics in these verses?

4. Choose a verse to memorize this week. Begin working on it now.

DAY 2—BEGIN IN PRAYER

1. Read Philippians 4:1–3.

2. Paul refers to the church at Philippi by several endearing terms in verse 1. Look up the definition of these words.

   a. Brethren

   b. Beloved

   c. Joy

   d. Crown

overFLOWING joy

PHILIPPIANS 4:1-9 — **LESSON #10**

3. Paul reminds those he loves at Philippi (and us) to **stand fast in the Lord**. What do we learn from the following verses about standing fast?

   a. 1Corinthians 15:58

   b. Galatians 5:1

   What tools do we have access to which enable us to stand fast?

   a. Ephesians 6:10-18

   b. 2Peter 1:5-8

4. Paul exhorts those in the body to get along and to encourage one another in their service toward the Lord. According to the Word, if we have a disagreement with someone, it is ***our*** responsibility to go and try to reconcile. What do the following Scriptures teach us about reconciliation, forgiveness and our responsibility to walk in unity?

   a. Matthew 5:23, 24

   b. Matthew 18:15-17

c. Mark 11:25

d. Romans 12:16-20

Personal: Do these verses bring to mind someone that you have an unresolved problem with? Do you need to forgive someone who has wronged you? Does Paul's exhortation to the ladies at Philippi need to be applied directly to your life? If the answer is yes, ask the Lord to give you a heart of obedience to His Word.

5. In today's lesson, what *instructions* do we need to follow? What *warnings* must we heed? Are there any *promises* we can rest our faith upon?

6. Close your study time in prayer asking the Lord Jesus to make any necessary changes in your heart, mind and attitude this week!

DAY 3—BEGIN IN PRAYER

1. Read Philippians 4:4-5.

2. The word *"rejoice"* is the expression of joy. Joy is one of the virtues of the Christian life. It is the fruit of the Spirit and can only be experienced by those who have the Spirit within them. Joy is not the same as happiness. Happiness is based on circumstances and dependent upon feelings. Joy is based on the truth of Who God is, what He has done for us and what He will do. These truths **do not change**. What do the following verses teach us about the Lord and why we have every cause to *"rejoice in Him* **always**"?

a. Isaiah 41:10

PHILIPPIANS 4:1–9 — LESSON #10

b. John 3:16, 17

c. John 15:13–16

d. 1 Peter 2:9, 10

3. Moderation means forbearance, gentleness, and sweet reasonableness. Paul is saying that we ought not to be unduly rigorous about unimportant matters. We are to be flexible in our dealings with one another realizing that God is able to affect every necessary change that is required in each of our lives. What encouragement and **reminders** do we receive from these verses?

a. Galatians 5:26–6:2

b. 1 Peter 4:8, 9

c. 1 Peter 5:5, 6

d. James 5:8, 9

PHILIPPIANS 4:1–9 — LESSON #10

4. The greatest source of encouragement to unity is this truth: *"the Lord is at hand."* We are to live each day as if it will be the day of His return. The following Scriptures give us warnings and encouragement regarding this attitude of expectation. What do they say?

   a. Matthew 24:45–51

   b. Romans 13:11–14

   c. 1 Thessalonians 5:6–9

5. In today's lesson, what *instructions* do we need to follow? What *warnings* must we heed? Are there any *promises* we can rest our faith upon?

6. Close your study time in prayer asking the Lord Jesus to make any necessary changes in your heart, mind and attitude this week!

DAY 4—BEGIN IN PRAYER

1. Read Philippians 4:6–7.

2. The word translated *careful* in verse 6 means *to be anxious or troubled*. In Greek it means *to be pulled in different directions*. Our hopes pull us in one direction; our fears pull us in the opposite direction and we are pulled apart! The old English root word for *worry* means *to strangle*. Paul's solution to our worry is that we commit ourselves to prayer. What do the following verses teach us about prayer?

   a. Psalm 55:17 and 22

b. Proverbs 3:5–7

c. Luke 18:1

d. 1 Thessalonians 5:17, 18

3. Paul teaches us that through prayer, supplication and thanksgiving we can experience God's peace in our hearts. Look up the definition of these words and find the more specific meaning of each.

   a. Prayer (v. 6)

   b. Supplication (v. 6)

   c. Thanksgiving (v. 6)

   It has been said that a person's knees cannot tremble with worry and anxiety if he is kneeling on them in prayer!

4. In verse 7 we are told that when we come to God in prayer we will experience God's peace which passes understanding and this peace will guard our hearts and minds through Christ Jesus. The **source** of worry and anxiety is our heart **(*wrong feelings*)**, or our mind **(*wrong thinking*)**. So, if we come to the Lord in open communication, asking Him to meet our needs and surrender to His

will in thanksgiving, He promises to guard our hearts and minds. What more can we learn about His peace that passes understanding?

a. Psalm 29:11

b. Isaiah 26:3

c. John 14:27

d. John 16:33

5. In today's lesson, what *instructions* do we need to follow? What *warnings* must we heed? Are there any *promises* we can rest our faith upon?

6. Close your study time in prayer asking the Lord Jesus to make any necessary changes in your heart, mind and attitude this week!

DAY 5—BEGIN IN PRAYER

1. Read Philippians 4:8–9.

2. Make a list of the things that Paul instructs us to focus our thoughts and meditations upon. *"Whatsoever things are..."*

Can you give an example of something that is true, honest, just, pure and lovely?

Personal: Spend a few moments comparing this list with the things that have been occupying your thought life today. Is there room for refocusing the things you are thinking about? Commit yourself to self-discipline. Ask the Lord to remind you the moment your thoughts turn to that which does not please Him or edify you!

3. These thoughts are the things that must prevail in our hearts and minds if we are to grow spiritually. What do the following verses teach us about how we must guard and regulate the information that enters our mind and thereby affects our hearts?

   a. Psalm 1:1–3

   b. Psalm 19:9–14

   c. Psalm 119:9–11

   d. 1 Timothy 4:13–16

4. We are responsible to be obedient to the things we have learned about the Lord and His requirements for our lives. Paul begins to close the letter by saying, *"That which you learned, received, heard and seen in me—**now do**—and the peace of God will be with you."* Obedience is an absolute requirement in the lives of those who love the Lord. What more can we learn about obedience from these verses?

a. Matthew 7:21-27

b. John 15:12-15

c. James 1:21-25

d. 1 John 2:3-6

5. In today's lesson, what *instructions* do we need to follow? What *warnings* must we heed? Are there any *promises* we can rest our faith upon?

6. Close your study time in prayer asking the Lord Jesus to make any necessary changes in your heart, mind and attitude this week!

DAY 6—BEGIN IN PRAYER

1. Read Philippians 4:1-9.

2. List the lessons that you've learned this week.

PHILIPPIANS 4:1–9   **LESSON #10**

3. Will you allow the Lord to mold and change you into His image as you seek to walk as He walked?

4. How are you doing on your memory verse for this week? *If you do not remember it, work on it today.*

Be careful for nothing; but in every thing by prayer and supplication with thanksgiving let your requests be made known unto God. And the peace of God, which passeth all understanding, shall keep your hearts and minds through Christ Jesus. Philippians 4:6, 7

PHILIPPIANS 4:10–23 — LESSON #11

DAY 1—BEGIN IN PRAYER

1. Read Philippians 4.

2. Re-read Philippians 4:10–23.

3. What are the main topics of these verses?

4. Choose a verse to memorize this week. Begin working on it now.

DAY 2—BEGIN IN PRAYER

1. Read Philippians 4:10–13.

2. Paul rejoices over the material care the church at Philippi provided for him whenever they had opportunity. They had sent Paul a financial gift and evidently it was not the first, for he said, *"your care of me that flourished **again**."* What do we learn from the Word about our responsibility to provide for the needs of those who lack when we are able?

   a. Deuteronomy 15:7, 8

   b. Matthew 25:35–40

   c. James 2:14–17

   d. 1 John 3:16–18

PHILIPPIANS 4:10–23 — LESSON #11

3. In verses 11 and 12, Paul declares he is able to be content in whatever state he finds himself. (Remember: he is in prison awaiting word about his sentence—possibly death.) The word translated "abased" here is used elsewhere in the Greek language to describe a river in a time of drought. Paul knew not only the experience of having both very little and abundance, but he also had learned *how* to live in these circumstances. What do the following verses teach us about our need to learn how to experience this same contentment?

   a. Matthew 6:31–34

   b. Hebrews 13:5, 6

   c. 1 Timothy 6:6–9

4. How could Paul be content whether full or hungry? He anticipated the question and gave the answer in verse 13. The secret, he said, is Christ! He was able because he could do all things through Christ who strengthened him. So, then, how are we to achieve this contentment when we are constantly faced with the lure of the world and all of its stuff. Read John 15:1–11 and answer the following questions. (Do you recognize the truth of true contentment which Paul tells us he had learned?)

   a. Who is the vine? Who are the branches?

   b. List all that you learn about the branches.

PHILIPPIANS 4:10–23 — LESSON #11

c. What are the benefits of abiding?

d. Why did Jesus speak these things (v. 11)?

How then can we *learn* to be content in whatever state we find ourselves?

5. In today's lesson, what *instructions* do we need to follow? What *warnings* must we heed? Are there any *promises* we can rest our faith upon?

6. Close your study time in prayer asking the Lord Jesus to make any necessary changes in your heart, mind and attitude this week!

Day 3—Begin in Prayer

1. Read Philippians 4:14–17.

2. There were times in Paul's ministry when he had little or no support for his ministry. The Scriptures are clear about our responsibility to provide for those who preach and teach the gospel. What more do we learn from these verses?

   a. Matthew 10:7–10

   b. 1 Corinthians 9:9–14

PHILIPPIANS 4:10-23 — LESSON #11

c. Galatians 6:6

d. 1 Timothy 5:17, 18

3. The church at Philippi had faithfully remembered Paul in their giving, even sending gifts all the way to Rome. This display of love from a part of the Body of Christ so far away was a great encouragement to Paul. When we are led to give of our time, effort and money to the church and others who minister faithfully in the Word, what is to be the correct motive for our giving?

a. Deuteronomy 16:17

b. Matthew 6:1-4

c. Romans 12:8

4. In verse 17, Paul reminds the church at Philippi that his encouragement for them to continue in giving was for their spiritual benefit and blessing so *"that it may abound to your account."* What promises are given in these verses about the blessings of giving?

a. Proverbs 3:9, 10

b. Matthew 10:40-42

PHILIPPIANS 4:10–23 — LESSON #11

    c. Luke 6:38

    d. 2Corinthians 9:6–8

5. In today's lesson, what *instructions* do we need to follow? What *warnings* must we heed? Are there any *promises* we can rest our faith upon?

6. Close your study time in prayer asking the Lord Jesus to make any necessary changes in your heart, mind and attitude this week!

DAY 4—BEGIN IN PRAYER

1. Read Philippians 4:18–19.

2. The act of giving is an offering and an act of worship unto the Lord. It is a sweet-smelling sacrifice that is well pleasing to the Lord. Define the following words to give you a better understanding of the Lord's teaching to us regarding our giving.

    a. Sacrifice (v. 18)

    b. Acceptable (v. 18)

    c. Well-pleasing (v. 18)

PHILIPPIANS 4:10–23 — LESSON #11

3. What do we learn about the sacrifices of praise and worship from these Scriptures?

   a. Psalm 116:17

   b. Romans 12:1

   c. Hebrews 13:15, 16

   Personal: Does your life, your heart, your praise and giving reflect the offering that is a sweet-smelling sacrifice, well-pleasing to God? Will you allow the Lord to make your life more closely aligned with His heart? Ask Him now to make any needed changes!

4. God promises to supply **all our needs**. We do not need to worry, fear, or despair. We need to learn to trust in His abundant riches. How do these verses encourage and remind you to rest in God's promises and His provision for your every need?

   a. Psalm 55:22

   b. Psalm 127:1, 2

   c. Matthew 6:6–8

PHILIPPIANS 4:10–23 — LESSON #11

d. Matthew 6:25–32

e. 1 Peter 5:6, 7

5. In today's lesson, what *instructions* do we need to follow? What *warnings* must we heed? Are there any *promises* we can rest our faith upon?

6. Close your study time in prayer asking the Lord Jesus to make any necessary changes in your heart, mind and attitude this week!

DAY 5—BEGIN IN PRAYER

1. Read Philippians 4:20–23.

2. Paul closes his letter in praise to our Heavenly Father Who is the **only** One Who is deserving of our honor, praise, and glory. Look up the following verses and record what we learn about those things that bring glory to God.

    a. Matthew 5:16

    b. John 15:8

    c. Romans 15:5–7

©2001—MORNINGSTAR CHRISTIAN CHAPEL, WHITTIER, CA

PHILIPPIANS 4:10-23 — LESSON #11

d. 1Corinthians 6:19, 20

3. Paul could see this church he greatly loved in his mind's eye. He ends his letter with a greeting of encouragement to the body at Philippi. He probably didn't know them by name, but he knew the importance of each one of them to the Lord and to His work. How do we, as members of the family of the Lord, strengthen and encourage one another?

a. John 13:34, 35

b. John 15:12, 13

c. 1John 4:7, 8

Personal: How are you doing at showing your love for the Lord and others by meeting the needs of the Body of Christ at your church? What if everyone in your church was loving to the same degree you are? Would your church be a better place to fellowship or not?

4. Paul refers to each of the believers as saints. He salutes all the saints at Philippi and sends greetings from the saints in the household of Caesar. This statement gives us some insight into Paul's ministry even from jail and how the Word of God had transformed the lives of those with whom Paul had contact. If you have trusted Christ Jesus as your Savior and Lord, then you are a *"saint"* according to the Word of God. (If you have not yet asked the Lord into your heart, today is the day of salvation.) What do we learn from these verses about the life of the saint?

©2001—Morningstar Christian Chapel, Whittier, CA

PHILIPPIANS 4:10-23 — LESSON #11

a. 1 Corinthians 1:2-6

b. 1 Corinthians 6:1-3

c. Ephesians 2:19-22

d. Ephesians 5:1-4

5. In today's lesson, what *instructions* do we need to follow? What *warnings* must we heed? Are there any *promises* we can rest our faith upon?

6. Close your study time in prayer asking the Lord Jesus to make any necessary changes in your heart, mind and attitude this week!

DAY 6—BEGIN IN PRAYER

1. Read Philippians 4:10-23.

2. List the lessons you've learned this week.

PHILIPPIANS 4:10–23   LESSON #11

3. Are you filled with joy? Do you have the mind of Christ? Are you gaining in the knowledge of Christ? Are you walking in the peace of Christ? It is quite possible and I encourage you to put this letter into practice daily in your life.

4. How are you doing on your memory verse for this week? *If you do not remember it, work on it today.*

I can do all things through Christ which strengtheneth me.
Philippians 4:13

May the Lord richly bless you as you continue to seek Him through His Word. May you be filled with joy unspeakable and full of glory as you learn to love Him more deeply, follow Him more closely and obey Him more fully!

Now unto Him that is able to keep you from falling, and to present you faultless before the presence of His glory with exceeding joy, to the only wise God our Savior, be glory and majesty, dominion and power, both now and ever. Amen. Jude 1:24, 25

Made in the USA
Columbia, SC
07 August 2024